CW01045744

MIXED MARRIAGES

THE REVISED DIRECTORY
PROMULGATED BY THE BISHOPS' CONFERENCE
OF ENGLAND AND WALES
30TH APRIL 1990

*All booklets are published thanks to the generous support
of the members of the Catholic Truth Society*

CATHOLIC TRUTH SOCIETY
PUBLISHERS TO THE HOLY SEE

CONTENTS

INTRODUCTION

The Catholic Church in England and Wales recognises that the question of 'mixed marriages' is a very important one, and one that raises a number of delicate ecumenical and pastoral issues. The Church's policy concerning marriages between Catholics and those of other faiths or none was clearly spelt out by the late Pope Paul VI in a *Motu Proprio "Matrimonia Mixta"* in 1970. Since then a new *Code of Canon Law* has been promulgated by Pope John Paul II. It seems appropriate now for the Bishops of England and Wales to revise the Directory which we first published in 1970 and revised in 1977. We are aware that this Directory is concerned with only one aspect of some marriages, namely a difference of faith between the partners. We are equally aware of the need for pastoral guidance concerning the Sacrament of Marriage, preparation for marriage and the Church's support for those who are married[1].

The years since 1970 have seen steady progress in the search for unity between divided Christians. The visit to this country by Pope John Paul II in 1982 was remarkable not least for the warmth of the welcome given to the Pope by so many of our Christian brothers and sisters from other Churches. It was the Pope himself who described this country as a 'special ecumenical terrain'. The continuing dialogue between the Catholic Church and the other Christian Churches in this country has helped to create a new ecumenical situation and a commitment to grow into full unity[2]. This should be reflected in our approach to so important a question as mixed marriages.

Episcopal Conference of England & Wales

---

[1] The Department for Christian Life and Worship has published a programme for pastoral guidance in 'Briefing' (Vols 17,12; 18,11; 19,1; and 20,1).
[2] cf. The Final Declaration issued by Church leaders at the Swanwick Conference, 1987 (in "Churches together in Pilgrimage" BCC/CTS 1989).

MIXED MARRIAGES

At the outset it is important that we should distinguish clearly between different kinds of 'mixed marriage'.

'Neither in doctrine nor in law does the Church place on the same level a marriage between a Catholic and a baptised non-Catholic,[3] and one between a Catholic and an unbaptised person; for, as the Second Vatican Council declared, those who, though they are not Catholics, "believe in Christ and have been properly baptised are brought into a certain, though imperfect, communion with the Catholic Church". Moreover, although Eastern Christians who have been baptised outside the Catholic Church are separated from communion with us, they possess true sacraments, above all the Priesthood and the Eucharist, whereby they are joined to us in a very close relationship. Undoubtedly there exists in a marriage between baptised persons, since such a marriage is a true sacrament, a certain communion of spiritual benefits which is lacking in a marriage entered into by a baptised person and one who is not baptised.' (*Matrimonia Mixta* (*MM*) Paul VI, 1970)

The question has been asked as to the appropriateness of the term 'mixed marriage' to describe a variety of different situations. Pope Paul VI was himself well aware of the problems created by this particular term. In many parts of the world it is used to describe marriage between members of different races. It is widely used in that sense in Britain. Even in its religious use it refers indiscriminately to widely different marriages. On the one hand it refers to the marriage of a Catholic to a non-baptised person or to someone who, although baptised, is not an active member of any Church. On the other hand it also refers to the marriage of two practising and committed Christians. It is obviously important to make the distinction very clear. The suggestion has been made many times that the more appropriate term to describe the second kind of marriage would be 'inter-church marriage'. In the course of

---

[3] This phrase, 'non-Catholic', is a translation from the Latin texts cited and is used in a number of places throughout this document. We apologise to those who may not consider it the most suitable term.

4

this Directory we would want to recognise the particular pastoral needs of such 'inter-church marriages', and we would be anxious to show the same pastoral sensitivity that Pope John Paul expressed in his address at York in 1982:

'In your country, there are many marriages between Catholics and other baptised Christians. Sometimes these couples experience special difficulties. To these families I say: You live in your marriage the hopes and difficulties of the path to Christian unity. Express that hope in prayer together, in the unity of love. Together invite the Holy Spirit of love into your hearts and into your homes. He will help you to grow in trust and understanding.'

Whilst we shall consider both the problems and the opportunities created by a genuine 'inter-church' marriage, we must recognise that in our pastoral practice such marriages are very much the exception. The vast majority of our marriages could not properly be described as 'inter-church'. It is our duty also to give clear guidance in this Directory to those involved in mixed marriages where this ecumenical dimension is missing.

The reason why we still make use of the general term 'mixed marriage' to cover these widely differing situations is that we are part of a world-wide communion, and that we have a great deal of international correspondence about marriage cases of one kind or another. Great confusion could be caused if we were to adopt our own purely local terminology with regard to marriage.

THE CHURCH'S BASIC ATTITUDE

The Church has always had a special care for those who enter the married state, both in the preparation of those couples for marriage and in supporting their Christian family. The Church speaks of the family as 'the domestic Church', and is well aware that unity within the family is always something vital to the stability and development of that marriage. There are so many factors today which militate against that vital unity that the Church is naturally worried about blessing a union where religion itself might become a source of division.

The Church therefore has a special concern for marriages between Catholics and persons of other Christian traditions or other faiths. Experience shows that certain problems arise in many mixed marriages.

In our society mixed marriages are more than ever likely. The days when Catholics lived apart from the rest of society are over, and we have become used to living in a society where men and women of different races, cultures and traditions mix together. The changing patterns of society are bound to be reflected in the experience of the Church.

It is against this background that we, as bishops, must offer pastoral guidance to the priests and people in our care.

PASTORAL GUIDANCE

Preparation for marriage is part of a much larger programme of preparation for life, and as such it is the duty of priests, parents and our Catholic schools. It is very important that those who bear such a responsibility help young people to see some of the difficulties that can be experienced in mixed marriages as well as some of the hopes and joys where spouses share a deep and living faith.

It is crucial that our young people are recognised by us as 'The Church of Today' as well as the 'hope of tomorrow'. They will need to discover their own role within the life of the Church if they are to be able to identify with the Church and grow in faith. Our main concern should be to develop mature and committed young Catholic Christians, who know their faith and love it. In so far as we are able to achieve this we can at least hope to be able to point out the practical problems inherent in any mixed marriage.

It is worth emphasising how important it is for the priest or deacon[4] to adopt a positive attitude to those who come to arrange a marriage. The bishops' advice on this matter in the 1970 Directory bears repeating:

'When, however, people come to the priest to arrange for a marriage they have decided to enter into...it is almost always too

---

[4] Throughout this Directory, when the word 'priest' appears, if appropriate, it could also refer to a deacon.

late to attempt to dissuade them. It is then much more important for the priest to remember that this is possibly the non-Catholic's first personal contact with a priest, and that he, as a priest, can contribute considerably to the present and future happiness of the couple...by his kind, welcoming attitude. He is a minister of Christ's Gospel to everyone. He has an opportunity here to build up the spiritual life of both young people in preparation for their marriage. If this is his mind, his attitude will be truly pastoral....'

Writing in 1970, Pope Paul VI spoke of the Church's duty of discouraging mixed marriages, and of the Church's clear preference that 'Catholics be able in Matrimony to attain to perfect union of mind and full communion of life'. At the same time the Pope was at pains to point out that men and women have a natural right to marry and beget children, and that the Church must ensure that her laws do justice to the demands of God's law and to the right to enter into marriage in accordance with God's law. The points stressed by Paul VI are equally valid today, and will remain so. In entering into marriage the Catholic partners must be reminded of the conscientious obligation they have of doing nothing to imperil their own faith, of doing all that they can to pass on that faith to their children, and of respecting the conscientious convictions of their partner in marriage. For those Catholics who have lapsed from the practice of their faith, this will provide a valuable opportunity for priests to rekindle in them the gift given at their baptism.

PREPARATION FOR MARRIAGE

If a couple preparing to enter marriage are to be helped to appreciate what these obligations mean, it will be necessary to offer them real and effective pastoral care. Pope Paul VI believed that the Church must show her concern 'both in preparing for marriage those who intend to contract such a marriage and in caring for those who have already contracted such a marriage'. This must involve giving them 'a sound knowledge of the Christian nature of marital partnership'.

We would certainly share this concern, and would want to encourage the priests and the parish communities who are involved in the pastoral care of marriage to use the opportunity afforded by the wedding to encourage the understanding, belief and practice of the Christian faith in both bride and groom.

Pope Paul emphasised the need for pastoral watchfulness and skill. Commenting on this, the bishops in 1970 wrote as follows: 'In England and Wales there is an admirable tradition of systematic home visitation of all Catholics by the clergy of the parish. To this we attribute in great measure the spiritual health of the Catholic Community. Certainly, wherever it is neglected signs of stagnation and decay quickly show themselves.' Nearly twenty years later the scene has changed somewhat. The community is involved at every stage of preparation for the sacraments, and candidates meet to explore together the step they are taking. Preparation for the sacrament of marriage is increasingly being undertaken in this way. It can be very effective in providing the 'pastoral watchfulness' which Pope Paul regarded as so important.

We should just like to add that many newly-weds do not receive the pastoral care that would help them in the first months of their married life because the priest and people of the parish in which they make their new home do not know of their presence. It is good that they should be visited and welcomed by them, and introduced to members of their parish who will support them in the practice of their faith. For this reason some priests, in the course of preparing people for their marriage, enquire where they are going to live when they are married so that they can let their future parish priest know in advance of their arrival. We emphatically recommend this practice for all marriages. In some dioceses this practice is now of obligation.

JOINT PASTORAL CARE

In the 1970 Directory, the Bishops spoke of the value of joint pastoral care of the couple entering into a mixed marriage. In the case of an 'inter-church' marriage, namely one in which both partners are practising members of their own Church, such joint pastoral care seems to be crucial. Pope John Paul II's words at York in 1982 about such couples living in their marriage 'the hopes and difficulties of the path to Christian unity' clearly imply that the partners will need to deepen their own faith, and their own knowledge of their faith, and that each will need to be strengthened by God's grace in the living out of that commitment. Each will be entitled to look to his or her respective pastor for real assistance in their vocation.

The strength and support which a partner who belongs to a different Christian tradition may draw from his or her own community of faith can enrich immeasurably the life of a family in a mixed marriage. It would obviously be very desirable that the Catholic priest should work as closely as possible with other clergy involved in the couple's preparation for marriage and in subsequent support of that Christian family. The difficulties which this may involve must be recognised honestly, so that realistic attempts are made to overcome them. This will demand a high degree of commitment from all those concerned, but it constitutes a telling sign of the Churches' concern for the unity of the Church, especially of the 'domestic Church'.

The Catholic Church's understanding of itself and its convictions about who may and may not be admitted to the Eucharist can and do create problems. Christian Unity is now a central concern of the Catholic Church. Work for ecumenism cannot be regarded as an 'optional extra' for Catholics. At the same time no progress will be made unless we are able to recognise that there are still serious matters which divide us, and that we must not ignore the sincerely held convictions of one another. The Catholic Church's attitude to the Holy Eucharist and our inability to allow all who wish to do so to share with us in receiving Holy Communion undoubtedly cause pain and distress to many other Christians. We recognise that this is so, but we have to ask them to appreciate that this discipline is a reflection in practice of the Catholic Church's self-understanding. The link between the 'Body of Christ' which is the Eucharist and the 'Body of Christ' which is the Church is a very profound one. We hope that our common study of these difficult questions may lead to a deeper understanding of the nature of the Church, and in so doing bring nearer the day when we can come together united in faith at one Eucharist.

Meanwhile the particularly acute problems in this area which face couples in a genuinely 'inter-church marriage' are going to require a real pastoral and ecumenical sensitivity on the part of the clergy involved. It will be necessary to encourage such couples to accept Pope John Paul's advice mentioned above:

> 'Together invite the Holy Spirit of love into your hearts and into your homes. He will help you to grow in trust and understanding.'

We are anxious to emphasise the fellowship of all the baptised. We are concerned that our pastoral practice in England and Wales should reflect that unity which we already enjoy and the spiritual benefits which flow from it. In some places Catholics and Christians of other traditions combine in organising preparatory courses for those intending to marry. Joint witness to Christian principles of marriage before, at, and after the wedding, within the home and in public, is eminently desirable in this as in many other ways.

Catholic teaching and Catholic law have always recognised an important difference between the marriage of a Catholic with another baptised Christian and marriage with a person who is not baptised. The first is a Christian sacrament, the second is not.

It will be noted in the norms promulgated in this Directory that the new *Code of Canon Law* has reinforced still further the difference between these two kinds of marriage. 'Mixed religion' (i.e. where both partners are baptised) is no longer referred to as an impediment to marriage requiring a dispensation, whereas 'disparity of worship' (i.e. where one partner is unbaptised) is an invalidating impediment, which does require a dispensation from the local Ordinary (cf. Norms 1 and 3).

The Church also makes a liturgical distinction between the two kinds of marriage (cf. Norm 9).

In the case of an unbaptised person belonging to another faith, it will be helpful to ensure that he or she understands the Christian vision of marriage. It is also important that the Catholic partner should understand something of the faith of the non-Christian. For example, when a Catholic is planning to marry a Muslim it is necessary for the Catholic to be clear about the Islamic view of marriage and its practical implications. Pastoral problems can arise if the couple are intending to live in an Islamic country.

The regular meetings between the priest and the couple before the wedding will provide an occasion for dialogue. The couple may never have discussed their respective faiths with each other, and this might be an excellent way of deepening their knowledge of each other and of deepening their unity. They may come to discover how many values they share. It would be difficult to overstate the importance of such a dialogue at this crucial time in their relationship or of the need to encourage couples to pray together.

In the case of a person with little or no religious background, even if they have been baptised, the meetings between the priest and the couple before the wedding can offer a chance to commend the Christian vision of marriage, and very often to re-awaken an interest in the Christian faith. It is wise to recognise that more and more of the young people who come to us for marriage have little or no idea about the Christian faith. It would be foolish to imagine that even the most basic Christian truths are widely known or understood. Moreover many young people will come with entirely mistaken notions of the Church's teaching. They can be greatly helped if the priest takes care to explain the Church's deep love and concern for those entering marriage in terms that they can understand. This is an opportunity for evangelization and he should avoid giving the impression that the Church's concern is narrowly legalistic. He should never declare the law of the Church without explaining its pastoral purpose.

THE OBLIGATIONS OF THE CATHOLIC PARTNER

Mixed marriages in modern society are always likely to bring to the surface the differences between the Catholic understanding of marriage and that of others. Among Christians there may well be differences about the nature of marriage as a sacrament, the importance attached by the Church to the celebration of marriage within the Church, and about certain moral principles pertaining to marriage and the family. These questions can only be fully resolved when Christian unity is restored. Meanwhile it is necessary for Catholics to be fully aware of the teaching of the Church in these matters as well as being sensitive to the different views of other Christians.

Where a marriage takes place between a Christian and an unbaptised person these differences may well be far more radical. In practice the same will often be true where the other partner has been baptised but has no actual experience of Christian faith or practice. It is wise to anticipate that in both these cases the Christian view of marriage may well be entirely unfamiliar.

When two people are planning to get married they are often much more open to the influence of God's grace. The experience of being in love is one that touches people very deeply. For this reason it is sometimes possible to awaken memories and to sow seeds of faith in a way that would not otherwise be possible. The Catholic understanding of marriage as a sacrament can speak in a very real way to people preparing for marriage. The idea that in their love for each other they can catch a glimpse of the powerful love of God is one that can have an appeal for them. It is an opportunity for the priest to try to deepen the faith of the Catholic partner, and to alert the other partner to the seriousness with which the Church approaches marriage.

The Catholic partner must be helped to understand that although the discipline of the Church may change in particular circumstances, there are still obligations which flow from Divine Law. In so far as a particular discipline is seen as an expression of Divine law it is something on which the Church must insist. The Church can change laws which she has made as a matter of simple discipline, but she cannot change what she has received from God as Divine Law. Thus the requirement of the Church that Catholics should marry according to 'Canonical Form' (i.e. in the presence of a priest and two witnesses) is a matter of Church discipline, and can be dispensed by the Church for serious reason. However, the requirement that marriage be accepted as a life-long union of two people in love and fidelity is an expression of the teaching of Christ himself, and can never be altered. The same is true of the duty to preserve one's faith:

> 'The faithful should therefore be reminded that the Catholic partner to a marriage has the duty of preserving his or her own faith; nor is it ever permitted to expose oneself to a proximate danger of losing it.' (*MM*)

Pope Paul's words here express the Church's conviction that faith is a precious gift from God, and that no one is free to enter into a marriage that would involve a grave risk of losing one's faith. On the other hand, decisions as to how this obligation applies to particular individuals rest with the Church.

> 'Furthermore, the Catholic partner in a mixed marriage is obliged not only to remain steadfast in the faith, but also, as far as possible, to see to it that the children be baptised and brought up in that same faith and receive all those aids to eternal salvation which the Catholic Church provides for her sons and daughters.' (*MM*)

Both the new *Code of Canon Law* and the *Motu Proprio* of Paul VI in 1970 make it clear that 'the Catholic is obliged as far as possible to see to it that the children are baptised and brought up in the Catholic Church'. These words attempt to express two important convictions on the part of the Church. In the first place, the Church is concerned that Catholics should clearly understand their God-given duty to do all in their power to hand on to any children they might have the precious gift of their Catholic faith. If we believe that faith is a gift from God, and that through our faith we have been given an insight into God's truth and his purposes for the world, we cannot in good conscience turn away from the truth. Thus individual Catholics must recognise a God-given obligation to do all that is possible to preserve their own faith and to pass on that faith to their children.

13

In the second place the Church is concerned to show proper respect for the beliefs and convictions of others. It is not possible to spell out in precise detail how each couple will solve the problems that sometimes arise when the sincere beliefs and convictions of each partner are in conflict. It is, however, necessary to insist that those who are about to enter into marriage should recognise and face up to their responsibilities in this area.

The Church has chosen at different times to approach this delicate question in different ways, and that is perfectly proper. It is for the Church to decide how best to ask the Catholic partner to acknowledge this responsibility. At the same time it is necessary to make the point that the responsibility itself comes not from church law but from the fact perceived by the Catholic faith that the Catholic Church is not simply one church among many but central to the plan of salvation instituted by Christ. While other Christians may not share that conviction, they would not expect us to deny our deepest beliefs about the nature of the Church willed by Christ. This is at the very heart of the ecumenical problem. At the same time they would certainly expect us to be sensitive to their beliefs and that our practice would be sensitive to their convictions also.

'The problem of the children's education is a particularly difficult one, in view of the fact that both husband and wife are bound by that responsibility and may by no means ignore it or any of the obligations connected with it. However, the Church endeavours to meet this problem, just as she does the others, by her legislation and pastoral care.' (*MM*)

Prior to Pope Paul VI's *Motu Proprio "Matrimonia Mixta"* of 1970 the partner from a different Christian tradition or another faith was required to give an undertaking to assist the Catholic in the religious upbringing of the children of the marriage or at least to do nothing to impede it. Such partners are no longer required to make this positive commitment. At the same time, however, it is necessary to avoid giving the impression that the Catholic upbringing of the child can be entirely separated from its general upbringing. To bring up a child as a Catholic involves much more than simply fulfilling those obligations that fall on the Catholic partner such as baptism, religious instruction and Sunday Mass. It must involve the whole of life. The beliefs, attitudes and example of both parents will inevitably have a profound influence on the total formation of the children. Thus both partners have a duty to cooperate with each other in the general upbringing of the children. The experience of many couples shows how the fulfilment of even such specifically Catholic obligations as Sunday Mass can be greatly helped by a co-operative attitude on the part of the Catholic's partner in very practical ways.

This is not to put undue pressure on the Catholic's partner, but simply to recognise that the Catholic partner's promise to 'do all that I can within the unity of our partnership' to have all the children baptised and brought up in the Catholic faith, will inevitably be affected by the other partner's attitude. He or she will necessarily make an important contribution to the education and upbringing of the children which the Catholic may not exclude.

At this point we would want to lay special emphasis on the positive contribution to be made by those partners in a mixed marriage who belong to a different Christian tradition or adhere to another faith. They will certainly recognise for themselves an obligation to do all that they can to pass on to their children their own deeply held religious convictions. If these convictions are directly opposed to the Catholic faith, then questions should be asked about the wisdom of such a marriage. In practice it will often be the case that whilst such partners are unable to share fully in the faith of the Catholic, finding some aspects of our faith difficult to accept, they will usually find a great deal in common between us, and will want to build on that unity which already exists. The change in wording of the promise in the norms which follow attempts to ensure that the other partner does not feel completely excluded by the terms of the Catholic partner's promise. Both the liturgy of Marriage and of Baptism acknowledge this shared responsibility on the part of both parents. Both partners have a vital role to play within the marriage as father or mother, and as husband or wife. The wording of the promise is intended to recognise this fact and welcome the contribution made to the marriage by both partners.

THE CHURCH'S NORMS

The Norms given in this Directory are taken from the new *Code of Canon Law*, which came into force on 27th November 1983.

1. Without the express permission of the competent authority, marriage is prohibited between two baptised persons, one of whom as baptised in the Catholic Church or received into it after baptism and has not defected from it by a formal act, the other of whom belongs to a church or ecclesial community not in full communion with the Catholic Church. (Canon 1124)

There are two important changes in the Church's legislation contained in this canon.

a. 'Mixed Religion' is no longer referred to as an impediment requiring dispensation. What is required is the express permission of the competent authority, that is of the local Ordinary. Without that permission, a marriage would be unlawful (contrary to the authoritative prohibition of Christ's Church), but not invalid (null and void). It should be noted however that a marriage between a Catholic and another baptised Christian celebrated without the required permission of the Ordinary may be invalid if there is a defect of canonical form. (cf. Norm 5 below).

This canon should be seen as an expression of the Church's pastoral concern that the inevitable problems involved in any mixed marriage should be fully understood, and that every effort should be made to enable the couples to face up to the implications of a mixed marriage.

b. The Church's legislation now takes account of those Catholics who have defected from the Church by a formal act. Such persons are not now obliged to observe Canonical form. However they do require permission to marry Catholics as such marriages are now considered to be mixed marriages. (cf. Canons 1086, 1071#2)

The *Code of Canon Law*, however, does not define what constitutes a formal act of defection. The fact that a baptised Catholic has not practised the faith for some considerable time

16

would not in itself constitute a formal act. Such an act would have to involve a specific renunciation of the faith or formal admission to another church or sect. A person who has defected from the Church by a formal act is therefore not bound by the canonical form of marriage, and is presumed to be validly married provided he or she has been through a form of marriage recognised by civil law.

In cases where there is any doubt the priest should seek guidance from the local Ordinary.

2. The local Ordinary can grant this permission if there is a just and reasonable cause. He is not to grant it unless the following conditions are fulfilled:

1° the Catholic party is to declare that he or she is prepared to remove dangers of defecting from the faith, and is to make a sincere promise to do all in his or her power in order that all the children be baptised and brought up in the Catholic Church;

2° the other party is to be informed in good time of these promises to be made by the Catholic party, so that it is certain that he or she is truly aware of the promise and of the obligation of the Catholic party;

3° both parties are to be instructed about the purposes and essential properties of marriage, which are not to be excluded by either contractant. (Canon 1125)

The previous *Code of Canon Law* (1917) required a 'grave cause' to justify a dispensation. The New Code requires a 'just and reasonable cause' and, following the decree *Christus Dominus* of the Second Vatican Council, establishes that a dispensation can be given in particular cases to the faithful whenever it is judged by the competent authority that 'it contributes to their spiritual welfare' (cf. Canons 87#1 and 88). The same criterion of the spiritual welfare of the parties would certainly apply in cases which do not require dispensation but a simple permission. A 'just and reasonable cause' should not be interpreted in a negative sense only. Whilst the danger of a civil marriage or the danger of the Catholic party lapsing from the faith may certainly be a just and reasonable cause for granting such permission, at the same time the Code clearly suggests that positive reasons could also be put forward. Thus the spiritual maturity of the couple and their ability to face up together to the difficulties of a mixed marriage would also be a just and reasonable cause for granting the required permission.

1° The declaration and promise of the Catholic partner. (Canon 1125#1)

The obligation referred to in these canons is seen by the Church as an obligation arising from the law of God.

The Church, because of her pastoral responsibility to those preparing for marriage and her concern for the future of the children of such marriages, requires the declaration and promise to be made by the Catholic partner. She believes this to be her duty to Christ before she can give approval to a mixed marriage. Priests should explain this carefully to the couple.

We must obviously insist again that the promise concerning the children must be sincere. It is a sincere and deliberate undertaking 'to do all that I can', that is to say, all one can do in the actual circumstances of the marriage, without jeopardising the marriage, within the unity of the marriage.

We wish to make it clear that the other party is not required to give any undertaking in this matter, formally or informally. He or she must of course be informed of the Catholic's declaration and promise (cf. 2 below).

We strongly advise that a couple contemplating marriage should agree before the wedding about the baptism and education of any children they may have, and the priest should encourage them to do this. This however should not be used as a means of requiring of the Catholic's partner an assurance which the law does not require.

Problems can indeed arise if the Catholic's partner is determined to prevail upon the Catholic to abandon his or her faith, or is determined that the children (or some of them) shall be baptised and brought up outside the Catholic Church. This problem is acute when the other party adopts this attitude from conscientious conviction. In these circumstances the priest should discuss the problem in a friendly and helpful manner, for it is often the case that such attitudes are due to a misapprehension about the Catholic faith or some unfortunate impression from the past, and if these can be cleared away, an understanding can be reached. But if the attitude of the Catholic's partner remains so closed to the Catholic baptism and education of all the children that it makes nonsense of the Catholic's undertaking to do 'all that I can', then the matter must be referred to the local Ordinary because the need to refuse permission or dispensation may well have arisen.

Similarly, it has been known, although very rarely, for Catholics to suggest that their children both be Catholics and also belong to the denomination of their partner. This is not possible. It may be necessary to explain to both partners the theological reason for saying this. 'The Church' is not a purely abstract title to be given to all who believe in Christ. It is a visible community, which gathers regularly to worship God, a community whose unity is expressed in a variety of ways. By baptism a child is received into that visible community. So long as the sad but real divisions remain between Christians it is unrealistic to think of trying to bring up children in two distinct communities. Where both parents are active and committed members of different churches it is very likely that their children will be involved to some extent in both, but it is necessary for them to belong to one or the other.

But all this is to consider only the cases of difficulty, and even of extreme difficulty, in this matter. In our experience such cases are rare, and indeed usually arise from misunderstanding.

More commonly the person from a different Christian tradition generously co-operates in the Catholic education of the children. In this connection we think it is useful to bring two points to the attention of Catholics committed to marriage with such a partner. On the one hand, Catholic education means more than just sending the child to a Catholic school. What the children learn from their parents at home, and that from earliest years, is an even more important part of education. On the other hand, the truths of faith that their children learn from their parents are normally those truths which are common to all Christians. This means that there is a wide field of positive cooperation in the Catholic education of their children open to the conscientious parent from a different Christian tradition.

Such parents will normally find themselves at one with their Catholic partners in believing, and therefore at ease in together presenting to their children, nearly all of what is fundamental to the Catholic faith.

One thinks at once of the existence of God, our heavenly Father, the Creator of all, and our ability to communicate with him in prayer; the Person of Jesus his Son, who was born of the Virgin Mary and became one of us; his life and teaching as recorded in the Gospels; his call to us to become his by faith and baptism and Christian living; his saving death, resurrection and ascension; the dwelling of the Holy Spirit within those who love him; the joy of heaven to which this love leads; virtues such as kindness, honesty, truthfulness, obedience and respect.

This is the briefest outline. We think that many parents of differing Christian traditions who face their responsibility for the spiritual formation of their children will discover that the field in which they can co-operate in this aspect of their parenthood is much wider than they at first imagined.

Where the children, despite all the Catholic's efforts, are baptised and being educated in the faith of the partner, the promise made by the Catholic still has meaning. It demands that the Catholic partner: (i) intends to play an active part in the Christian life of the marriage and of the family: (ii) will do all that he or she can, in the actual circumstances of the marriage, to draw the children to the Catholic faith: (iii) will deepen his or her faith in continuing to study it, so as to have a fruitful dialogue with the partner on matters of faith, and be able to answer the questions of the children: (iv) will pray with the family, especially asking the grace of unity, as Our Lord willed it.

2° On informing the non-Catholic party about the promise and obligation of the Catholic party (Canon 1125#2)

We strongly recommend that the other partner be informed as early as possible of the' Catholic's obligations in conscience which are expressed and acknowledged in the declaration and promise. It is important that Catholics should be aware of their obligations in this matter long before they come to arrange their marriage. Those who are involved in teaching should ensure that these obligations are known and understood. A Catholic should indeed let such a friend know of these obligations as soon as the possibility of marriage enters into their relationship. The friend is thus as free as possible to withdraw from the association if he or she would find respect for such obligations intolerable.

3° Concerning the instruction to be given to both parties (Canon 1125#3)

This is not a requirement which is special to mixed marriages. It applies to all. The Prenuptial Enquiry form includes a reminder of the priest's duty to explain these points to all who seek marriage in the Catholic Church.

Canon 1063 reminds pastors of their obligation in this regard and of the importance of using every means available, including the church community, to see that marriage preparation is fruitful. Many dioceses will have their own programmes, in addition to any national initiatives (cf. footnote 1 on page 1). We require that a couple should be given at least four instructions, but this should be seen as an absolute minimum.

We recommend Sections 47 to 52 of the Second Vatican Council's *Pastoral Constitution on the Church in the Modern World* as a text from which engaged couples may be instructed on the Christian pattern for married life. What is being particularly insisted upon in this norm, however, is that people who are about to marry should know, and not exclude from their matrimonial consent, the elements essential to Christian marriage. These elements are:

i. the essence of the matrimonial consent itself, namely, the exchange of the right to sexual intercourse which is open to the generation of new life;

ii. the unity of marriage, namely that this right is to be exchanged with no other person during the lifetime of the other partner;

iii.the permanence of marriage, namely, that this right is intended to remain as long as both live.

3. A marriage is invalid when one of the two persons was baptised in the Catholic Church or received into it and has not by a formal act defected from it, and the other was not baptised. (Canon 1086#1)

This impediment is not to be dispensed unless the conditions mentioned in Canon 1125 and 1126 have been fulfilled. (Canon 1086#2)

Disparity of worship remains an invalidating impediment. Thus without a dispensation such a marriage would be null and void. Those who have formally defected from the faith do not require a dispensation to marry an unbaptised person.

By this law the Church continues to distinguish the marriage of a Catholic with an unbaptised person from the marriage of a Catholic with a person who, though not a Catholic, is a baptised Christian.

4. It is for the Episcopal Conference to prescribe the manner in which these declarations and promises, which are always required, are to be made, and to determine how they are to be established in the external forum, and how the non-Catholic party is to be informed of them. (Canon 1126)

In leaving it to the Episcopal Conference to determine the way in which the declaration and promise are to be made, Canon 1126 insists again that this declaration and promise are always required. The procedure we require is that, when the Catholic applies to marry a person from a different Christian tradition or another faith, the priest to whom he or she applies must obtain all necessary certificates and fill up a form which specifies:

i. The name, and religious allegiance of each of the two people who propose to marry, the parish of the Catholic, and the fact that the Catholic has applied to the priest for permission or dispensation.

ii. That the Catholic has given a declaration and promise (preferably in the presence of the other party) in the following words:[5]

'I declare that I am ready to uphold my Catholic faith and to avoid all dangers of falling away from it. Moreover, I sincerely undertake that I will do all that I can within the unity of our partnership to have all the children of our marriage baptised and brought up in the Catholic Church.'

The Catholic can choose to give this declaration in one of two ways: either:

a. The Catholic partner signs the above declaration contained in the appropriate form in the presence of the priest who also signs as a witness.

or

b. The Catholic partner makes the above declaration verbally in the presence of the priest who then signs a statement on the appropriate form confirming that this has been done.

iii.A statement by the priest that the declaration and undertaking have been explained to the Catholic's partner and indicating whether they were made in the presence of that person.

---

[5] or their substantial equivalent, to be determined by the diocesan Bishop.

iv. A statement by the priest that in his opinion the other partner will not oppose the Catholic's fulfilment of his or her declaration and promise in such a way as to make them meaningless.

v. A statement given by the priest that the four required instructions have been given.

vi. A statement by the priest of the just cause or causes which apply.

vii. The priest's signature to a declaration that all the statements made by him on the form are true.

In most dioceses in England and Wales, the Bishop delegates Deans (Canon 553#) and parish priests (Canon 515#) to grant permission for a marriage between a Catholic and a baptised Christian from another tradition, and to grant a dispensation *ad cautelam* from the impediment of disparity of worship only in those cases in which there is a serious doubt about either the validity or the fact of the baptism. There are three exceptions to this delegation:

Deans and parish priests are not delegated for the convalidation of invalid marriages,
nor when the Catholic refuses to make the declaration and promise,
nor when the opposition of the other partner is such as to render the declaration and promise of the Catholic meaningless.

Note:

i. No Dean or parish priest is obliged to use this faculty that is delegated to him. He may always, if he wishes, apply to the local Ordinary.

ii. The '*ad cautelam* clause' is the only case in which the faculty to dispense from an invalidating impediment is delegated.

iii. To avoid possible difficulties, there is a grave obligation on those who have this faculty to use it only for their own people.

iv. If it seems to the Dean or parish priest that he must refuse permission, the whole matter must be referred to the local Ordinary.

v. Parishes in the dioceses concerned are provided by the diocesan curia with a book of forms for granting these permissions, and providing a copy of each. This should be produced for inspection at the time of Visitation of the parish and must be returned to, and filed by the diocesan curia when it is full and a new book is applied for.

vi. No permission may be granted without completing the forms provided.

vii. The marriage of a Ukrainian Catholic and a person not in full communion with the Catholic Church, to be valid, must be performed according to the Ukrainian Rite. In this case the local Latin Rite Catholic Bishop and priests have no jurisdiction. All applications in the case of mixed religion and disparity of cult must be submitted to the Apostolic Exarchate. (22 Binney Street, London W1Y 1YN.)

5. The provisions of Canon 1108 are to be observed in regard to the form to be used in a mixed marriage. If, however, the Catholic party contracts marriage with a non-Catholic party of Oriental Rite, the canonical form of celebration is to be observed for lawfulness only; for validity, however, the intervention of a sacred minister is required, while observing the other requirements of law. (Canon 1127#1)

By the 'form' of marriage is meant the formalities required for that public expression of consent by which the contract of marriage is made. Norm 9 will speak of 'liturgical form'. Here Canon 1127#1 is dealing with 'canonical form', namely the formalities required by the law of the Church.

These are that in all normal circumstances, when a Catholic is being married, the exchange of consent must be made before a properly authorised Catholic bishop, priest or deacon, and two witnesses. Canon 1108#1 states: 'Only those marriages are valid which are contracted in the presence of the local Ordinary or parish priest or the priest or deacon delegated by either of them, who, in the presence of two witnesses assists....'

25

This requirement was introduced to eliminate the confusion which arose when people could claim the status of being married simply on the grounds that they had agreed together, even tacitly, to accept one another as man and wife. But even now, when the civil law eliminates this confusion, by demanding the registration of all marriages, the Church still insists upon canonical form. She does so for a pastoral and for a theological reason.

The **pastoral** reason is that by this regulation every Catholic being married will be in touch with a Catholic priest who will then be able to offer all the pastoral help the Church provides.

The **theological** reason in the case of marriage with another baptised person is that marriage is a sacrament. A sacrament is a sacred sign entrusted by Christ to his Church. In Christian marriage we see a living sign of Christ's love for his Church. Through this sacrament the human love of husband and wife becomes a sign of that undying faithful love. In receiving this sacrament the bride and groom receive from Christ the assurance of his constant presence with them and his help for them in their new life together. Because she sees the sacrament of marriage as so sacred, and because she is so deeply concerned, the Church desires that her members confer and receive it before her accredited minister. Even when a non-baptised person is involved, marriage remains sacred and so the Church wishes it to be celebrated before her minister.

In the marriage of a Catholic with a partner of Oriental Rite not in full communion with the Catholic Church, for validity it is sufficient for such a marriage to take place in the presence of a sacred minister of that partner's Rite, but for lawfulness it is required that the Catholic party obtains the permission of his or her own local Ordinary for the marriage to take place without canonical form (cf. the Decree of the Sacred Congregation for the Eastern Churches *Crescens Matrimoniorum*).

In the marriage of a Catholic with a Western person from another Christian tradition, the Church requires canonical form if she is to recognise the marriage at all. In such cases canonical form is required for validity.

Normally speaking, therefore, the wedding of a Catholic must take place in a Catholic church-building, and before a properly authorised bishop, priest or deacon and in the presence of two witnesses. This should be clearly explained to all Catholics. It should also be made clear to those who are not Catholics, and especially those who are contemplating marriage with a Catholic. Popular over-simplification has led to a widespread impression that the Catholic Church is now indifferent as to whether a Catholic marries before a Catholic priest or not. As the next norm will insist, a serious reason is necessary for a bishop to dispense from canonical form.

If there is difficulty about a marriage being celebrated in a Catholic church-building, the local Ordinary can, for any good reason, allow the wedding to take place in some other suitable place, such as a building belonging to another Church or ecclesial community. The permission, simply with regard to the place of the wedding, supposes that it will nevertheless be conducted by a properly authorised Catholic bishop, priest or deacon. There are legal difficulties with regard to making this arrangement in Anglican churches, but it has sometimes proved an acceptable arrangement in other churches.

6. If there are grave difficulties in the way of observing the canonical form, the local Ordinary of the Catholic party has the right to dispense from it in individual cases, having however consulted the Ordinary of the place of celebration of the marriage; for validity, however, some public form of celebration is required. It is for the Episcopal Conference to establish norms where this dispensation may be granted in a uniform manner. (Canon 1127#2)

For serious reasons the Catholic Church is willing to waive her demand that her members marry before a Catholic bishop, priest or deacon, properly authorised for the purpose, and two witnesses.

The element we would emphasise concerning this norm is that people should know both that the local Ordinary can dispense from canonical form, and that a serious reason is required for him to do so. It would be wrong for a priest to withhold this information. It would also be wrong for him to present petitions for dispensation where no serious reason for it exists. The dispensation cannot be given simply and solely because the couple would like it.

Reasons for granting dispensations from canonical form should concern in some important way:

i. The spiritual well-being of the parties, especially if the non-Catholic party is attached to the familial faith;

ii. The tranquillity and peace of their personal or family relationships;

iii.Or be based on the special relationship that the non-Catholic party has to a minister or non-Catholic place of worship.

The power to grant a dispensation from canonical form is in the hands of the local Ordinary of the Catholic party. If the proposed marriage is to take place outside his diocese, he is required by Canon 1127#2 to consult the Ordinary of the place of the celebration before granting the dispensation.

If a dispensation from form is granted, for validity some public form of celebration is required (Canon 1127#2). Care must be taken that the requirements of both canon law and civil law be fulfilled.

7. In regard to a marriage contracted with a dispensation from the canonical form, the local Ordinary who granted the dispensation is to see to it that the dispensation and the celebration are recorded in the marriage register both of the curia, and of the proper parish of the Catholic party whose parish priest carried out the inquiries concerning the freedom to marry. The Catholic spouse is obliged as soon as possible to notify that same Ordinary and parish priest of the fact that the marriage was celebrated, indicating also the place of celebration and the public form which was observed. (Canon 1121#3)

The change of procedure introduced by Canon 1121#3 should be noted. When a dispensation from canonical form has been granted and the wedding is to take place outside the home parish of the Catholic partner, the marriage documents are to be kept and filed in the Catholic's home parish. When the marriage has taken place, it is to be entered in the marriage register of the Catholic's home parish (not, as hitherto, in the Catholic parish in which the marriage was celebrated).

The priest must inform the Catholic partner before the marriage of his or her obligation to let him know as soon as possible after the marriage that it has taken place. He will need to have the appropriate details to enter them in the parish records. Providing a copy of the Marriage Certificate would be the practical way of fulfilling this obligation. Canon 1121#3 also requires that the marriage be recorded in the diocesan curia. The obligation to inform the curia belongs strictly to the Catholic partner of the marriage, but in practice it would be better for the parish priest to forward the required information to the curia.

It should here be noted that the Military Ordinariate has no canonically erected parishes; thus there are no parish records. All canonical acts (e.g. baptisms, confirmations, marriages, etc.) must be registered at the Ordinariate Records Office (St Michael's House, Queen's Avenue, Aldershot, Hampshire GU11 2BY). Hence, when a dispensation from canonical form has been granted by the Military Ordinary, the marriage documents are preserved at the Records Office, which applies to the place of marriage for a certificate, registers the marriage and notifies the place of baptism.

8. As soon as possible after the celebration of a marriage, the parish priest of the place of celebration or whoever takes his place, even if neither has assisted at the marriage, is to record in the marriage register the names of the spouses, of the person who assisted and of the witnesses, and the place and date of the celebration of the marriage; this is

to be done in the manner prescribed by the Episcopal Conference or by the diocesan Bishop. (Canon 1121#1)

A marriage which has been contracted is to be recorded also in the baptismal registers in which the baptism of the spouses was entered. (Canon 1122#1)

If a spouse contracted marriage elsewhere than in the parish of baptism, the parish priest of the place of celebration is to send a notification of the marriage as soon as possible to the parish priest of the place of baptism. (Canon 1122#2)

The above regulations apply to all marriages, including mixed marriages, celebrated in the Catholic Church.

It is the parish priest's responsibility to ensure that all marriages are recorded in the parish marriage register. It is also his responsibility to see that the details of a marriage are entered in the parish baptismal register of the Catholic spouse. When sending notification of a marriage to a spouse's parish of baptism, a stamped addressed envelope should always be enclosed; a marriage file is not completed unless and until notification has been received from the parish of a spouse's baptism that the marriage has been recorded in the baptismal register.

As noted above, however, in regard to subjects of the Military Ordinariate all registers are kept at the ordinariate Records office. Thus marriages celebrated in Catholic military churches (Navy, Army or Air Force, at home and overseas) are registered at Aldershot.

9. ...in the celebration of marriage those rites are to be observed which are prescribed in the liturgical books approved by the Church, or which are acknowledged by lawful customs. (Canon 1119)

The Episcopal Conference can draw up its own rite of marriage, in keeping with those usages of place and people which accord with the Christian spirit; it is to be reviewed by the Holy See,... (Canon 1120)

These Canons call attention to the appropriate forms of service given in *The Marriage Rite*, the new rite for the celebration of marriage[6]. The liturgical texts drawn up by the Bishops' Conference of England and Wales, in accordance with Canon Law, and approved by the Holy See, are to be used in all the dioceses of England and Wales.

These liturgical norms laid down by the Bishops' Conference, and approved by the Holy See, exclude the rite for the celebration of marriage within Mass when one of the partners has not been baptised. Diocesan Bishops have given general consent to the celebration of this rite within Mass whenever the Catholic's partner is a baptised person and when, taking all the circumstances into account, it seems appropriate to the couple and to the priest who is to preside at the wedding. However it may not always be appropriate to use that rite. If there is present in the congregation a large number of people belonging to different Christian traditions, the fact that they cannotparticipate fully in the Mass needs to be considered. They should, however, be invited to participate as fully as they can and the priest should encourage them to do so. The question is one that should be thought about carefully by the couple concerned and discussed with the priest. He should exercise his prudent pastoral judgement in advising them about this.

It may be helpful to point out that the rite for the celebration of marriage outside Mass is a full Catholic marriage liturgy. An unbaptised person might feel unhappy at being restricted to this rite. This problem can be overcome when the possibilities of the rite are explained. The fact that the Mass is not being celebrated need not mean that the ceremony will be unimpressive. Additional prayers and hymns can easily be added to the service as the couple wish.

Within the appropriate rite, the detailed choices of prayers and readings should be made by the couple with the priest who is to preside at the wedding. Most priests will already have experienced how helpful the joint consideration of all

---

[6] A further revision of The Marriage Rite is under way at the time of publication of this Directory.

these prayers and Scripture passages can be in deepening the couple's understanding of the sacredness of the covenant of marriage into which they are entering. This is specially true when the partners are not very well informed about the Christian faith.

When a Nuptial Mass is celebrated at a mixed marriage, the Church's law with regard to Eucharistic Communion must be observed. This law is contained in Canon 844 of the New Code.

10. It is forbidden to have, either before or after the canonical celebration in accordance with #1, another religious celebration of the same marriage for the purpose of giving or renewing matrimonial consent. Likewise, there is not to be a religious celebration in which the Catholic assistant and a non-Catholic minister, each performing his own rite, together ask for the consent of the parties. (Canon 1127#3)

When the marriage takes place before a Catholic priest or deacon, the appropriate Catholic rite referred to in Norm 9 must be used.

If the couple wish, and the parish priest consents, a minister from another Christian tradition may be invited to be present, in 'choir dress', on the sanctuary, and he may also be invited to take part in the wedding ceremony.

If the wedding is in a Catholic church according to canonical form, the Catholic priest or deacon must always perform his essential role as president at a marriage by receiving the matrimonial consent of both bride and bridegroom and by ensuring that the civil requirements are fulfilled. He should also reserve to himself enough of the rite for it to be evident that he is presiding. But he may certainly invite the other Christian minister to read passages from Scripture and prayers which are part of the Catholic rite. He may also invite him to give an address.

When, with dispensation from canonical form, the wedding takes place in a non-Catholic church or chapel, the rite of the wedding will presumably be that of the church or chapel in which it is being celebrated. Although in no way legally necessary, it might be appropriate in these circumstances that the Catholic priest or deacon who has been preparing the couple for marriage should, where possible, be present at the wedding. If invited to do so by the couple, with the consent of the minister in charge of the church, a Catholic priest or deacon may attend on the sanctuary, in 'choir dress', and, if further invited, take part in the ceremony provided it is not part of the eucharistic liturgy, just as a non-Catholic minister may be invited to take part in a Catholic rite.

What is forbidden by Canon 1127#3 is the simultaneous performance of different rites, or the addition of any second rite which includes the giving or renewal of matrimonial consent. This is a measure of simple prudence, to ensure that consent is expressed only once, and so possible doubts about validity are excluded. We positively recommend a second service of blessing and thanksgiving in the church of the other party, provided it does not include the giving or renewing of matrimonial consent. It provides this other party with the opportunity to give witness to his or her new responsibilities before the Christian community to which that person belongs.

11. Local Ordinaries and other pastors of souls are to see to it that the Catholic spouse and the children born of a mixed marriage are not without the spiritual help needed to fulfil their obligations; they are also to assist the spouses to foster the unity of conjugal and family life. (Canon 1128)

The provisions of Canon 1127 and 1128 are to be applied also to marriages which are impeded by the impediment of disparity of worship mentioned in Canon 1086#1. (Canon 1129)

Couples who have entered into a mixed marriage have a special call on the pastoral care of the Church community and of the clergy. There can often be pastoral difficulties for such couples, and they are entitled to look to the Church for pastoral care. This responsibility can only be met fully when the whole parish community is involved in the support of marriage and family life.

Mixed Marriages

In the case of marriage between a Catholic and a person from another Christian tradition, this pastoral care should be given whenever possible in co-operation with the clergy of the Catholic's partner. This, in turn, presupposes the sincere openness and enlightened confidence in the Ministers of other religious communities which we must work to establish.